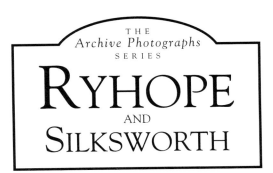

THE
Archive Photographs
SERIES

RYHOPE
AND
SILKSWORTH

The "Beauties" of Ryhope cannot be exaggerated. Too busy to write.

A somewhat romantic view of Ryhope from a postcard of the pre First World War period. The same drawing was probably used to depict any number of places by the simple expedient of changing the name on the caption and signpost. The models are, understandably, anonymous.

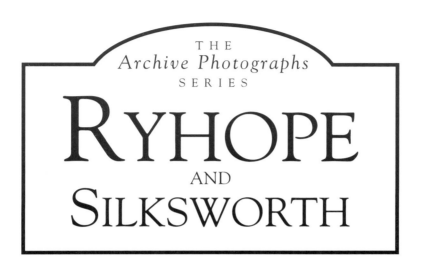

THE
Archive Photographs
SERIES

RYHOPE
AND
SILKSWORTH

Compiled by
J.N. Pace and Andrew Clark

CHALFORD

First published 1997
Copyright © J.N. Pace and Andrew Clark, 1997

The Chalford Publishing Company
St Mary's Mill, Chalford,
Stroud, Gloucestershire, GL6 8NX

ISBN 0 7524 1001 6

Typesetting and origination by
The Chalford Publishing Company
Printed in Great Britain by
Bailey Print, Dursley, Gloucestershire

Contents

Silksworth Junior School football team, 1958-59. Back row, left to right: Snowdon, Dixon, Richardson, Robinson, Brydon, Norman, Pigg. Front row: Mr Kirk (headmaster), Moore, Page, Cuthbertson, Crabtree, Smith, Mr Gormley. This was a very successful season for the boys. They were League champions, winners of the RAOB cup and runners-up in the Hedworth cup.

Acknowledgements

The authors would like to thank: Alan Brett, Peter Gibson, George Nairn, Ian Wright, Pat O'Brien, Alex Murray, Phil Hall (Sunderland Local Studies Library), Northeast Press, Vaux Breweries.
The authors also appreciate the co-operation of Ron Gormley in supplying Silksworth Junior School football team photographs and information.
Jim Pace particulary wishes to thank all who have contributed old photographs and information relevant to people, places and events in both villages, over the past thirty-five years. He also expresses his appreciation of the professional help and guidance of Andrew Clark, of Chalford Publishing, his co-author.

Bibliography

Alan Brett, *Sunderland Football Annuals*, 1990-96
Jim Pace, *Ryhope in Old Picture Postcards*, 1985
Ron Gormley and Aidan Tasker, *Schools' Football In Sunderland*, 1993
Tony Whitehead, *The Londonderrys of Seaham*, 1995

Introduction

This book does not attempt to be a history of the villages of Ryhope and Silksworth. Such a venture would be much better entrusted to local organisations dedicated to the necessary research, and with deeper local knowledge. It would be more appropriate to describe it as an account of people and their lives in the two communities over the past century or so as is recorded in photographs. If, in places, it is apparently incomplete, this is due to the lack of photographs to hand. I hope that the selection chosen, from several thousand items, will inform and entertain, and at the same time, awaken many memories.

It would be true to say that this book had its beginnings fifty years ago when I returned from war service in the army, and replaced Mr T.P. Leith, who was then retiring from the staff of the recently renamed Silksworth 'Modern' School, under its newly-appointed head, Mr N. Wilson. The year was 1947 and the shortages of wartime were still with us. Photography was very restricted at first, as films were virtually unobtainable by amateurs. As they gradually made their appearance, I became absorbed by the hobby. Much essential equipment had to be bought second-hand or made at home. My first enlargements were done on an enlarger made from off-cuts of wood begged from the local undertaker! However, it was a consuming interest which, alongside teaching, helped to bridge the gap experienced by most returning ex-service personnel, between Forces life and the civilian world.

In time, I found a special interest in old photographs and ways of copying them. I began with a few done to put on a show in the Ryhope Miners' Welfare Hall to attract attention to their Arts and Crafts Exhibition in the late 1950s. They were an immediate success, and, from that small beginning, the collection grew – and grew! With the support of the Ryhope Community Association, it now comprises several thousand items, forming a resource for residents, schools, students and even TV researchers. It also provided all the pictures for the commemorative wall in the Ryhope Health Centre.

In 1960, with the assistance of my pupils at the time at Silksworth Modern School, I made up a classroom display of some 200 photographs of that village. This was put on show in the local library, and again, some years later. Some of those pictures now form the basis of this book. While teaching, I photographed school events on an informal basis, and annually recorded the football, netball and cricket teams until 1973, when I left to become headmaster of Barnes Secondary School.

Over the years I saw many changes in school and village life. A good example was the advance of technology in the classroom. In 1947, it was a world of iron-framed desks with tip-up seats, inkwells (filled on Friday afternoons by two cheerful lads with blue-stained arms and hands) and chalk and talk. Around that time, I was asked to produce a school magazine in colour. There was no colour printing possible in those days within a meagre budget, but we succeeded, with the aid of a tin of gelatin and a process called hectographic duplicating. A master copy was made using a viscous coloured ink. This was laid upon a bed of gelatine. Then an image could be transferred and colour copies were peeled off. It was crude, but it worked for up to thirty sheets, after which a new master had to be prepared. Just to prove it could be done, we later did some four-colour work, using a table jelly from Woolworths. So much for technology! My last job, as a head master, was to order the latest computers for my school. There's progress for you!

The information given in this book is almost entirely dependent upon recollections of myself and my informants. While it is given in good faith, there is no guarantee of absolute accuracy. With class and team groups sometimes only a few names are given. This is not to exclude others, but simply to avoid overloading the reader with lists. Much of the pleasure of the pictures will be found in poring over them, perhaps in the company of others, discovering long-forgotten faces, and stirring, hopefully, happy memories of yesteryear.

I commend this book to the reader as a tribute to the lives of ordinary working folk in mining villages which have, in recent years, survived the trauma of losing their industry, and their secondary schools, to become absorbed into the greater unit of Sunderland. May they continue to survive, progress and prosper.

J.N. Pace, April 1997

One
Around Ryhope

Ryhope fire brigade station, c. 1910. The brigade originally had a horse-drawn engine and volunteer firemen had to first catch the horse. When Iley's the chemists had a fire, Sunderland's motorised fire engine arrived and put the fire out before the 'volunteers' 400 yards away turned out. The crew were largely members of Catholic families in those days and they were very proud of their training, duties and place in the community. They were equipped with uniform, belt, axe and rope. The building was recently converted to a youth club and appropriately named Blue Watch.

Ryhope pumping station was built in 1868 and was in use for almost a century. At the time it was constructed, it was an amazing engineering achievement. The beams for the pumping engines weighed 22 tons each and were supplied by Hawthorn of Newcastle. They had to be brought from Tyneside to Ryhope by teams of 40 horses. When they tried to cross the old cast-iron Wear bridge the toll-keeper refused permission for the journey, fearful of causing the bridge to collapse. The teamsters waited until dark, by which time the toll-keeper had gone off duty, cracked their whips and crossed the bridge. Whether they left the money for the toll does not seem to be recorded, but Ryhope got its pumping engine. The engine house building remained unfinished until the complete engine was assembled, then the walls were added.

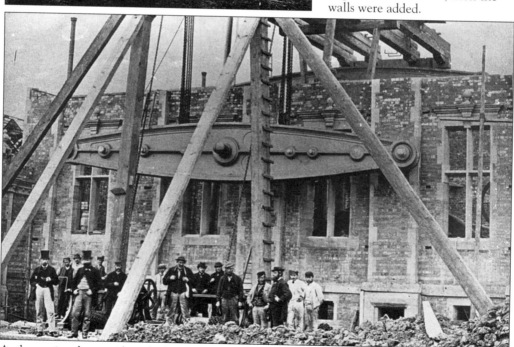

A closer view lets us identify the workmen. There are caps for the labourers and artisans, hats for the more skilled specialists, and toppers, for the managers and directors.

These rods transferred the rocking motion of the beams to the vertical motion of the pump, delivering 40,000 gallons an hour. The flywheels (seen left and right) weighed 18 tons each, and kept the pumping motion steady and continuous.

The viewing gallery in the engine house where the beams of the pumping engine can be seen gracefully and silently performing their operation. All parts of the engines can still be seen working thanks to the dedication of the Ryhope Engines Trust. It is especially fascinating on 'steaming' days when the smooth apparently effortless movements of the components are as impressive to visitors today as they were to their engineers well over a century ago.

The Green at the turn of the century, lined by lime-washed houses, inns and cottages. The standards holding the electric cables to power the trams date this scene to after 1905. In the centre, behind the tree, is the Forge, where horses were shod and farm machinery was repaired by the blacksmith. It is still in use as the Forge garage and filling station. Notice also the drinking trough, on the extreme right, to refresh passing horses.

By the 1890s gas lighting had been installed in the streets of Ryhope and a stone kerb protected the edge of the Green. The cottage on the Green was the residence of the Reeve, a medieval appointment usually held by a farmer, who was responsible for the letting of the common land to travelling fairs, showmen and gypsies. It was said to have had a stone upper floor, as a precaution against fires started by disgruntled people when disputes arose. The building was removed around the time of the First World War and the War Memorial now occupies the spot.

The road from Seaham via Ryhope to Sunderland, passing on its way the Mental Hospital, the General Hospital and the former Grammar School. Notice the large stones to mark its limits before proper kerbs were provided. It was originally only intended to take horse-drawn traffic, in contrast with today's heavy transport demands. The large house across the road is the second vicarage, built in 1898 to replace the original one which stood east of the Green on what is now the Seaham road. It is now the Old Vicarage nursing home.

Ryhope Street South in the 1960s. Beyond the shops is the site of the present car park of Kwiksave store. Further up the street are the large premises of Ryhope Co-op. The Kwiksave site was earlier known as the 'Rhubarb Field' and was, in fact, a source of market garden produce for the Co-op. The large gable end was the house of the general manager. On the right is the Colliery Welfare Hall, now the Community Centre.

Ryhope Hall, *c.* 1908. The front entrance stood where Cranston Place is now, and overlooked the Village Green at its Eastern End. It was the residence of Major Streatfeild, the owner of Ryhope Colliery. His son was well-known locally in his youth, and became a High Court judge, Mr Geoffrey Streatfeild QC.

The back garden of Ryhope Hall, *c.* 1908. Ryhope Hall had been, in the nineteenth century, a coaching inn on the Seaham to Sunderland route. It was frequently used by the gentry as a convenient hotel for enjoying sea-bathing. Legend associates it also with the highwaymen Turpin and Drummond but this is local gossip. The coming of the Londonderry, Seaham and Sunderland Railway (L.S. & S.R.) and the North Eastern Railway (N.E.R.) effectively ended the coaching days and the hall became the family home of the colliery owner, Major Streatfeild.

By the mid 1930s the Hall was a sorry wreck. It had served a variety of purposes from a wartime services canteen to a boys' club. Its ultimate demolition made way for Local Authority housing, now known as Cranston Place.

Ryhope Central Co-op Staff, *c.* 1914. They are in their working dress, which helps to identify their jobs. The grocers are in white, warehousemen in long, dark aprons, clerks in dark suits with collars and ties, and cartmen, horse-keepers and general labourers in caps and scarves. The managers wear starched white collars.

The women took over Ryhope Co-op in 1916 when the men were needed for the First World War. Many women were employed during the war due to the shortage of men. This was probably the first real step towards equal opportunities for women, though total equality took many years to materialise.

The Ryhope and Silksworth Industrial and Provident Society central premises in the 1960s. Owned by its members or share holders, it provided a diversity of goods and services, including all foods, fresh meat, bakery products, ladies and gents clothing, boots and shoes, banking and credit facilities, household supplies, furniture and even funerals. A dividend was paid to members every six months. Depending on profits, this could be as much as 20 pence in the pound. To families on low income this was a genuine bonanza and an occasion of great celebration. On 'Divi-day' there were generally presents for all the family.

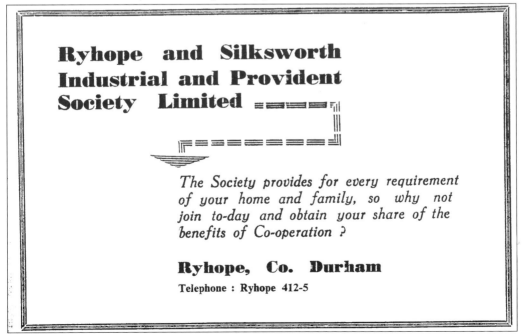

Ryhope and Silksworth Industrial and Provident Society Limited

The Society provides for every requirement of your home and family, so why not join to-day and obtain your share of the benefits of Co-operation ?

Ryhope, Co. Durham

Telephone : Ryhope 412-5

An advertisement for the Co-op, *c.* 1961.

The Toll Bar. This public house stands on the site of the Toll House and barrier across the Stockton Road, at which a toll, or fee, was charged for every person, animal or vehicle which crossed. The pub was often referred to as 'The Blood Kit' due to bare-knuckle fights which took place in the sand quarry behind. This sand pit was revealed when new housing was developed recently.

The Prince of Wales. Mining and farming were thirsty work and required adequate refreshment. Such premises were, and remain to this day, social centres of the population.

Ryhope had two stations and provided good rail contact with the rest of the county so it was chosen as the central site for a mental hospital, then called an 'asylum' or 'place of safety'. It opened in May 1895 to accommodate up to 400 patients and covered a tenth of the entire township at the time. On the neighbouring site in 1939/40 an emergency hospital was built in anticipation of wartime casualties. This developed into the present Ryhope General Hospital.

Ryhope School. With the village's two railway stations, Ryhope was also chosen as the most convenient site for the area's Secondary (later Grammar) School by the Durham County Education Authority in 1911. It was also in contact with Sunderland by electric trams and early buses. Pupils came from as far afield as Whitburn and Easington. Although no longer in use as a school, it is still recognizable today, although, a shadow of its former glory, functioning as a skills training centre.

RYHOPE OLD CHURCH. *(COPYRIGHT)*

Ryhope old church was built around 1826 with local farmers helping to transport large stones from the beach for its construction. It had a bell-cote and porch, and served the expanding village until the building of St Paul's church some forty years later. It then became the village's Church of England School, and the house on the left, originally for the curate, became the head teacher's. In more recent years the old Village School became the council rent office.

Church Ward, Ryhope, *c.* 1910. Church Ward is still a quiet backwater and looks little different after the passing of some eighty years. The house on the right was demolished in the late 1950s as was the one next door which long ago was occupied by the local doctor, Dr Gillan, whose son and daughter also gave years of service to the village. The large white house in the centre is 'The Wilderness'. This has a history which can be traced back to the sixteenth century. There is said to have been a brewery there but it would not have been like Vaux in Sunderland. It was probably only a stone out-building where ale was brewed for domestic consumption. This was a common practice in the days before a treated water supply. The ale had to supply family and servants.

Demolishing the '£5 houses', c. 1947. Local legend has it that the Coal Company built these houses at a cost of £5.00 each. Locally quarried stone was used to build the one storey houses and later an upper floor was added, with kitchens built at the rear. Many ultimately accommodated quite large families despite their size. Poor though miners undoubtedly were, they had a 'free' house, sufficient 'free' coal, as part of their wages, and generally a large garden for hens, pigs and fresh produce. But it was still a very hard life, working six days a week and no holiday pay.

A close up view of the bridge carrying the railway across Ryhope Beach Road. Lord Londonderry, having developed Seaham Harbour as his own port, wanted access to Sunderland docks also and developed the Londonderry, Seaham and Sunderland Railway (L.S. & S.R.) which was independent of the North Eastern Railway (N.E.R.). The iron bridge, which formerly crossed the coast road by the old convent, bore a marquis' coronet, and the bridge over the road to the beach still bears the letters L.S. & S.R. on the seaward side. Thus Ryhope was served by two separate railway companies, each with its own platforms and station master.

This house is believed to have stood on the south side of the Village Green, in the mid-nineteenth century. It was, at one time, occupied by William Wilton, a surgeon dentist, with a business at No. 53 John Street, Sunderland. A game of croquet is being played on the lawn by members of the family. The buildings on the right were later demolished and became the cattle mart. Hence the 'Farmers' Club' in the same area.

Town Farm, c. 1910. This farm at the east end of the Village Green was, like many other buildings, originally of locally quarried stone with a tiled roof. Just before the First World War several such houses were rebuilt in red brick with slate roofs. Notice the trees protected by iron ring fences. The Village Green of today owes much of its appeal to such foresight.

Two
Around Silksworth

These cheerfully fashionable young ladies of Silksworth Modern School in the early 1950s were typical of their age. Left to right: Laura Heslop, Elsie Forsyth, Hilda Longley, Pamela Ford, June Thompson.

Silksworth House. 3720

Doxford House. This impressive residence, originally set in spacious grounds, was for many years connected with the Doxford family, the famous Wear shipbuilders, who gave rise to the name of the nearby housing estate of Doxford Park.

The lodge of Silksworth Hall. The lodge and Silksworth Hall stand at the bottom of Botcherby's Bank. Notice the standards carrying the electric cables for the trams to Houghton and Sunderland. The figure in uniform seems to be a tramways official.

24

St Matthew's church. The church was an essential part of the development of the rapidly expanding colliery village, and in years past was very much the focus of village life. Along with St Leonard's Roman Catholic church and several chapels, it fulfilled both social and spiritual needs.

The mission room of St Matthew's in 1963. This was built by St Matthew's parish church as a communal meeting room for church and parish social events. In the late 1960s it was re-vamped as a youth club. In the grounds stood a wooden ex-army hut, used by the army cadets during the Second World War and later.

Mr Emmerson, as 'John Bull', leads the colliery band and decorated vehicles through Silksworth, passing the Miners' Hall in the late 1940s.

Blind Lane was widened in the 1920s to meet the increasing demands of motor traffic.

Silksworth Terrace. The photograph was taken from the corner of the former Junior School playground. In the distance is St Matthew's church, the former Silksworth Secondary (Modern) School and the Wynyard public house. The tram standards have gone, but in the centre, a gas lamp can be seen.

The Vane Arms. It was named, like many other pubs and streets in the area, after the Marquis of Londonderry's family, the Vane-Tempest Stewarts.

Tunstall Village, 1959. The snow ploughs were based there after a severe winter, and had been necessary to keep Ryhope Road and Tunstall Hope bank clear. Local farmers' tractors were used to pull them. (Photo Northeast Press Ltd, *Sunderland Echo*)

A rare picture of Tunstall Village, showing a tram passing through some time after 1906. It was a rural village of farmhouses at that time.

A tram at Silksworth at the turn of the century. The location is believed to be on the road towards East Herrington.

This was part of the rope-hauled wagon way that transported Lord Londonderry's coal from his pits in the Houghton/Rainton area to Sunderland across Warden Law. A stationary steam engine powered this until the 1950s. The watchman sheltered in the little brick house until it was time to open or shut the gates. It was believed to be in the vicinity of today's Gilley Law. When it closed, it was said to be the world's oldest rope-hauled railway.

The Village School was built by the Church of England and was a small school attended mainly by children of farm workers from the 1850s. It became a Board School by the 1870s and continued with around 50 pupils until the mid 1950s. It was then absorbed into Silksworth Junior School and the building was converted into a house.

In 1908 Councillor Palmer opened the newly built Silksworth Council School. The 'new' building at the other side of the playground opened in 1926. The school served generations of Silksworth children until the 1970s, when it was absorbed as an annexe of Farringdon Comprehensive School. It was closed some years later and demolished, with houses built on the site.

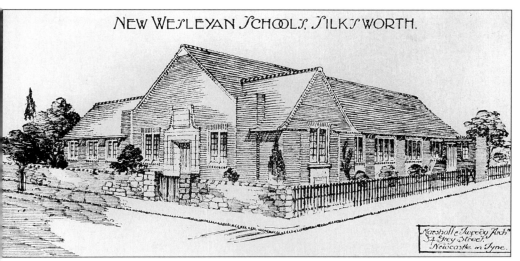

NEW WESLEYAN SCHOOLS, SILKSWORTH.

The New Wesleyan School, where a Sunday School was held. The building still serves Silksworth as the Weightman Memorial Hall. Opened in 1922 as a memorial by the local farming family, it has served as a place of worship and social centre for over 70 years. It is now the Methodist church.

Children admiring some artwork at an exhibition organised by the Silksworth Miners' Welfare Committee in the 1950s. Such events added much to the social life of the mining community.

Blind Lane in the 1950s. The impressive building in the centre was the Miners' Hall, the social,

trade union and political heart of the village. (Photo Northeast Press Ltd, *Sunderland Echo*)

Demolishing earth closets in Vane Street. The colliery houses were originally built with earth closets, commonly referred to as 'netties', which were emptied by the scavenger's cart each week. When sewers were laid, water closets were introduced.

The first 'refuse lorry' and crew in Silksworth. Having coal fires, most people burned their rubbish so bins did not get so full as nowadays. The crew worked very hard, lifting each bin shoulder high to empty it into the lorry. It was arduous, dirty, and often very smelly work and protective clothing was not provided by the Council in those days.

Three
Mining

A soup kitchen in Ryhope in 1932. Second from the right, in the light shirt, is Dick Jane, who in retirement was the 'Lollipop Man' for village schoolchildren. Soup kitchens ensured children were fed when miners were on strike.

Silksworth miners in the 1890s. The men are probably outside the lamp cabin where all safety lamps were checked and maintained. They wore no protective clothing as such, but are clad in stout boots or steel-shod clogs, thick woollen stockings, knee breeches and a variety of waistcoats and jackets. Their headgear is such as they would wear in the street and offers no protection in their workplace. They are all clean, therefore have not yet done their day's work. Pit baths were still half a century or more into the future.

Ryhope mechanics and blacksmiths, c. 1890. Sitting down, second from the right, is the son of John Walker who was made an apprentice in compensation for his father James, who was the first fatality at Ryhope. (See also p. 47). The man in the bowler hat, on the left, is Henry Johnson, colliery engineer and a pioneer member of the Ryhope Co-op Society.

A group of smiths and enginewrights from Ryhope Colliery, *c.* 1900.

Pit lads with 'bait' bags, *c.* 1930. There were no canteens in the 1930s and a man went to work with his tin bottle, filled with water or tea (a glass bottle might break). His sandwiches, pasty or whatever, being wrapped in a bag or bait poke. Different coal fields had their own vocabularies for such items. In some areas 'bait' was called 'snap' or 'piece'. Protective clothing, safety helmets and electric lamps were in the future for these lads.

Ryhope Colliery around the turn of the century. The winding headgear in stone and wood is clearly shown. Notice the untidy appearance of the place.

A clearer view from the opposite side. The headgear (pulley wheels) for the two shafts can be seen in the centre and to the right of the chimney. Two shafts were necessary for ventilation, and an escape route for trapped miners should one become accidentally blocked, as happened at Hartley Colliery in Northumberland, with a huge loss of life.

A view from the East. Notice the large reserve of timber pit props untidily stacked. This must be in the vicinity of the club house built for the golf course.

Erection of the new head gear at Ryhope in 1932. The old original stone towers, with heavy timber beams to carry the pulley wheels, were replaced with modern steel girders in this year. This was done during the Depression and a time of considerable unemployment to make the colliery safer, more efficient and more productive when economic conditions improved.

Silksworth Colliery. These photographs show it to be a tidy well-laid out site and not compressed between the sides of the valley as at Ryhope. The railway lines took coal via Tunstall Hope, past Hollycarrside, across the A1018 near the Forge Garage, to the main N.E.R. line and then on to Hendon docks.

As at Ryhope, the Silksworth Colliery site has been transformed for leisure pursuits, with lakes, sports fields, ski-slope, athletics track and tennis centre. These have replaced an industry which once employed almost 2,000 men.

Erecting the new winding gear at Silksworth Colliery in the 1950s.
(Photo Northeast Press Ltd, *Sunderland Echo*)

This was the development of a 'fan drift' at Silksworth Colliery, whereby foul air could be extracted from the shaft making the risk of poison gas and explosion much less. The lives of all men underground depended upon efficient ventilation. Men could not work in stifling conditions, and poisonous or explosive gases built up to dangerous levels in unventilated districts. Government regulations became extremely strict after many fatalities in the coalfields. The author's own grandfather was killed as a result of such a tragedy at Wingate Colliery in 1906.

Burning waste heaps, such as these at Silksworth, were a blight on many colliery villages. The sulphurous smell and smoke, occasionally even flames, spoiled many such places, as well as creating danger for unwary children, and considerable health hazards. Regular dumping of coal waste and furnace ash kept the fires going. They were finally controlled after the out break of the Second World War. The burning heaps provided easily identified markers for the enemy bombers and were doused with sprays of water pumped from the mine.

The colliery 'tankie', c. 1910. The tankie was the 'maid of all work' at the colliery. It needed no tender to carry water. It was stored in a 'saddle' tank over the boiler. A small amount of coal was carried behind the driver and fireman. Being short, it could easily negotiate quite sharp curves and for its size was very powerful for shunting long trains of coal trucks. The driver stands on the footplate and the man beneath is probably the fireman. The man on the right, with the long pole, uncoupled the trucks.

A team of stokers in the Ryhope Colliery boiler house. The furnaces, fire doors and boilers are behind them. The work was arduous and carried out in a very hot atmosphere.

Stokers in Silksworth boiler house, c. 1910. Steam was the source of power for winding engines, ventilation fans, pumping out water etc. This required fuelling and stoking of boilers, and the stoker's job was non-stop. Here a group pose in their working dress. The shovels look to have been specially polished for the picture.

Ryhope Colliery management and officials, 1923. 'Management' meant such people as manager, under-manager and agent. 'Officials' were over-men, deputies and chief clerks.

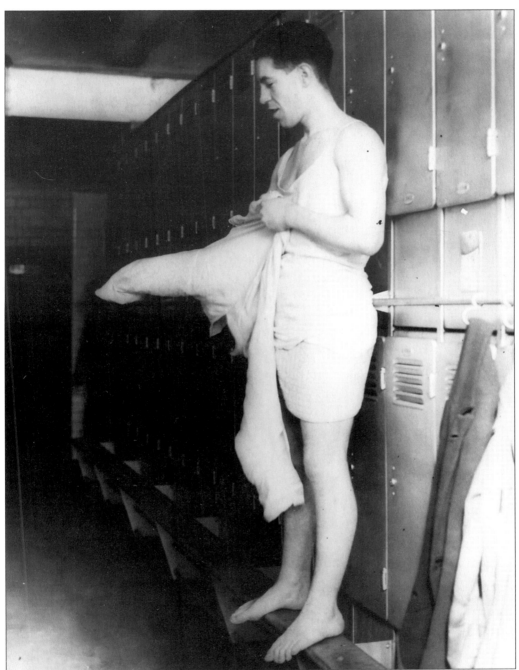

Silksworth pit head baths, 1939. Before this time men went home wet and blackened with coal dust. They bathed in a tin bath in front of the fire. Clothes had to be shaken and beaten clean out of doors, usually by the girls of the family, while boots were thoroughly dubbined to make them waterproof. Before the advent of pit-head baths, many of the older generation of miners *never* had their backs washed, maintaining that this weakened them! Instead, they had them dry-scrubbed with a piece of 'harn' (sacking). (Photo Northeast Press Ltd, *Sunderland Echo*)

Mine rescue team, *c.* 1920. Such rescue teams were made up of volunteers who were trained specially to handle the many ever-present dangers of mining. Poisonous gas was the most serious hazard, hence the breathing apparatus. Notice the overman, on the left, with his leather safety helmet and yard-stick which was used for many things, including tapping the roof to test it for safety. Leather protective helmets were just being introduced for senior officials.

Fire & Rescue Brigade. Photographed at Silksworth, this specialist vehicle and crew was available to all collieries in the area around 1913. Notice the uniforms, safety helmets and the spare tyre. The idea of a spare wheel had not come in yet!

In memory of John Walker who was killed falling down the shaft at Ryhope Colliery, 6 November 1860. He was 35 years old. Walker was the first of just over 100 men killed in 110 years of mining at Ryhope Colliery. He was buried in the village church yard. St Paul's was not built until several years later. His wife was presented with a mangle with which she could wring out neighbours washing for a penny or two a time. So much for compensation! Also, his eldest son was promised an apprenticeship at the colliery when he was old enough.

The miners' memorial in St Paul's church, dedicated by the Bishop of Durham in the late 1980s.

In 1892 a serious dispute at Silksworth between owners and workers resulted in striking miners being threatened with eviction. As the men no longer worked at the colliery, argued the owners, they were no longer entitled to live in colliery houses. Court orders of eviction were served by bailiffs and under police supervision, miners, families and all belongings were literally put out in the street. Feelings naturally rose very high and the bitterness created took years to pass. The episode was recorded in photographs by Mr Storey, then the owner of the *Sunderland Echo*.

Bailiffs carry out the court order. Striking miners sit on the roof to intimidate the bailiffs and demonstrate solidarity with the occupants.

The police, bailiffs and management reps. Some of the police were local men who must have found their duties rather odious. Baton charges resulted in many casualties among workers and families

An evicted family. Respectably dressed for the time, this family are facing homelessness and total loss of income. Vindictive, punitive measures were often suffered by strikers and their loved ones.

A Silksworth soup kitchen in 1921. During long strikes the miner's first priority was to ensure the children did not suffer unduly. With meat bones begged from local butchers and vegetables from their gardens, nourishing hot soup was served daily from tin baths to keep the children fed.

A rally during the 1926 strike. The actual location of this mass meeting is not recorded but it is believed to be in the Silksworth area. The speaker, in white shirt at the centre, must have had a powerful voice. There was no public address system in those days. At best he may have had a megaphone.

Wives and mothers lead a procession of over 1,000 in Stockton Road, Sunderland in 1932. The protest started in Ryhope with the march ending at Sunderland Police Court. The demonstration was over the 629 miners who had been summoned for alleged breach of contract after a dispute at Ryhope Colliery. The colliery probably had fewer strikes than most. The most serious was this one in 1932. The lady at the front with the hand bag was Councillor Dot Ridley, who gave many years of genuine service to Ryhope people.

Another soup kitchen, this time from the 1932 strike, outside Ryhope Infants School. George Lilley, third from the left in the back row, later became a prominent member of the Ryhope community and the Independent Methodist chapel.

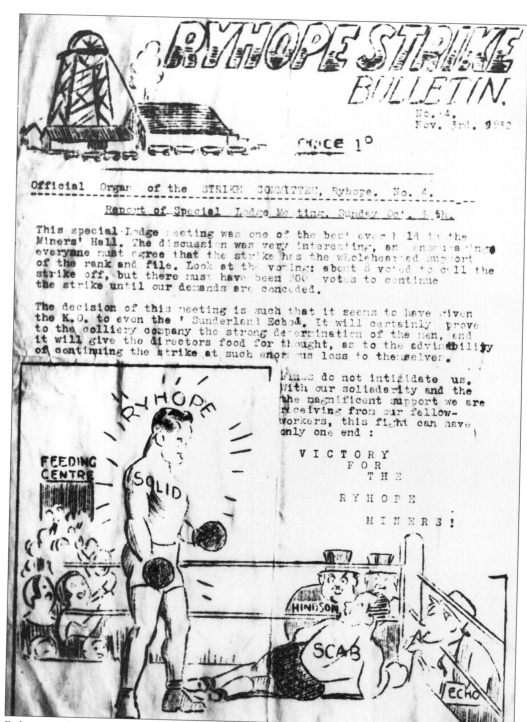

RYHOPE STRIKE BULLETIN.

No. 4.
Nov. 3rd. 1932

PRICE 1ᴰ

Official Organ of the STRIKE COMMITTEE, Ryhope. No. 4.

Report of Special Lodge Meeting, Sunday Oct. 30th.

This special Lodge meeting was one of the best ever held in the Miners' Hall. The discussion was very interesting, and encouraging everyone must agree that the strike has the wholehearted support of the rank and file. Look at the voting: about 8 voted to call the strike off, but there must have been 800 votes to continue the strike until our demands are conceded.

The decision of this meeting is such that it seems to have given the K.O. to even the 'Sunderland Echo'. It will certainly prove to the colliery company the strong determination of the men, and it will give the directors food for thought, as to the advisability of continuing the strike at such enormous loss to themselves.

Fines do not intimidate us. With our solidarity and the the magnificent support we are receiving from our fellow-workers, this fight can have only one end :

V I C T O R Y
F O R
T H E
R Y H O P E
M I N E R S !

Ryhope strike bulletin, 3 November 1932. The strike resulted in a series of bulletins to keep miners' families informed. In 1932 very few people had 'wireless' sets and newspapers tended to be rather biased, so leaflets such as this put the workers' point of view.

A master key such as this could open the simple lock of every colliery house in Silksworth. The 'key man' allocated houses to workers and held a position of responsibility and influence in the village.

Miners, 1925. Compare this with the 1890s photograph on p. 36. There is little change in dress. By manhood, most face-workers could be identified by their pale complexion, from lack of sunlight, and blue scars due to injury on the coal face. There were no pit head baths to clean up, and men went home black to wash in a tin bath in front of the fire, tended by their wives.

Training a pit pony at Ryhope Colliery. These sturdy little beasts spent much of their lives underground, 'putting' coal. They were first trained to be used to harness and tunnels underground.

Riversdale Terrace, Sunderland, in the 1920s. This is a coal delivery from Silksworth Colliery. The cart is a 'coop' cart and the horse is a Clydesdale. All domestic deliveries were made in one ton loads like this, usually from coal depots in town. Notice the cartman's leather leggings for protection. 'Coop' was a local dialect word meaning 'to tip' or turn over.

Four
Sport and Pastimes

A gym class from Silksworth Modern School, 1958. Members include Donaldson, Pearce, Maynard and Legge. The school had no gymnasium. All training was done in the school hall. Neither were there showers or changing rooms for pupils.

This is said to be a ladies team of the First World War period. We are not sure whether the nurses were needed for the players or the crowd. Notice the team appear to be wearing steel toe-capped pit boots.

Somebody Rovers', c. 1905. It is revealing to compare this group of young Ryhope footballers with their counterparts of ninety years later. Their only item of 'kit' was the football. Such pictures reflect the poverty of the time in mining villages, but it was poverty that refused to accept defeat. Ten years on most of them would be in the thick of the First World War.

Ryhope St Paul's FC, 1905. The trainer, on the left in back row, has the obligatory towel.

St Paul's CI football team, 1912-13. Linking church and sport, we have the St Paul's church institute team including the firmly positive vicar of Ryhope, Canon P.Y. Knight, third from the left in the back row. The goalkeeper is wearing the traditional flat cap.

Sunderland District Tramways AFC, 1920-21, included a number of Silksworth men.

Ryhope PM chapel football team, 1924-25.

Silksworth Colliery Welfare Junior football team, 1947-48. There are signs of post-war prosperity in the turn-out of this Colliery Welfare team.

Sunderland Boys v Deerness Valley, 29 October 1949. This match was in the English Schools' Shield competition of 1949 at Roker Park when Sunderland boys beat (hammered) Deerness Valley Boys 11-0. Billy Bainbridge scored six goals and George Lax got four. Both were pupils of Silksworth Modern School.

Peter Simpson, capped for county and England, in 1956. One of Silksworth's most successful schoolboy footballers, Peter played for England Boys v Scotland Boys at Wembley as centre half in 1956.

Bobby Gurney scores Sunderland's first goal in the 1937 Cup final.

Silksworth CW, 1920-21. Bobby Gurney is third from the left. Bobby, born in 1906, played for Bishop Auckland before signing for Sunderland in 1925. He then went on to become one of Sunderland's most famous players. The centre forward scored over 200 goals for his only professional club. The highlights of his career were; winning the League Championship in 1935-36 when he was joint leading goalscorer in the First Division; winning the FA Cup in 1937 when he scored one of the goals in the 3-1 win over Preston at Wembley; and appearing for England against Scotland in 1935. Mr Dodd, headmaster, stands behind Gurney in the playground of the Secondary School.

Silksworth weight-lifting team, in the Silksworth Senior School garden in 1920. There was a huge surge of interest in physical development after the First World War. The hut stood in the school garden at Silksworth until the end of the Second World War. The Health Centre now stands on the site.

The strong-man of Silksworth, R. Miller, champion weight-lifter, 1919.

Silksworth PM Gymnastic team, 1920. A team of ten members of the Silksworth Primitive Methodist church show their skills in a firm, well-constructed pyramid. Churches and chapels did much to encourage competitive sport and fitness and keep young people interested.

Tug-of-war was always popular as a 'fun' sport. This is an event at a Silksworth Modern School sports day in the early 1950s. Having no school field at that time, this annual event was usually held on the cricket field by courtesy of the Miners' Welfare Committee. The teachers, centre, are Mrs Robson and Mr Mason.

The Robinsons cricket team. All the players were related and from the same Silksworth family.

Co-op staff at the Ryhope Co-operative Butchers' Cricket Gala Day, 1912. Third from the left, standing, wearing a straw boater, is Nicol Harrison, who later became butchering manager. After the colliery, the Co-op was the largest single employer in the village. Such events as this were special to all ages, before the age of the wireless, cinema and television.

The presentation of the Monkwearmouth Charity and Wearside League Cups at the Miners' Welfare Hall, Silksworth for the successful CW football team in 1952.

The first ladies' bowls tournament at the colliery welfare greens. Notice the lack of standard footwear and dress, nowadays almost obligatory.

Ryhope prize band, 1929. Colliery bands were a great feature of the area and a source of much local pride. Competitions were strictly controlled and judged, and success was reflected in the morale of the entire village.

Miss Balderstone's elegant Scottish dancing group in the mid 1950s. Left to right: Marjorie Tait, Vera Holt, Betty Bell, Iris Beaney, Maureen Cuthbertson, Pauline Forrest, Constance Rodgers and Sylvia Brown. The group would dance to a wind-up gramophone, with no amplifier, and a duration of three to four minutes per winding.

Silksworth Orchestra, 1917. Many working folk found entertainment in musical pursuits. They took their practice very seriously and performed whenever an audience could be found. This was long before the days of LP records, tapes and CDs. Even the radio was still some ten years in the future. The violin was popular on account of its compact size. In some homes, organs and pianos had pride of place.

Ryhope Amateur Operatic Society, c. 1932. Further proof of the cultural pursuits of mining communities was the rise of operatic societies. Ryhope Co-op Hall provided the venue for annual gala performances and regular concerts. Such events helped raise public morale during the Depression years of the early 1930s and also raised funds to support local charities.

David Brown of Silksworth, even as a youth in the late 1950s, was keen on training racing pigeons, and proudly brought his trophy to school. Not bad for a thirteen-year-old.

Derek Forth, c. 1950. Derek, a Silksworth school prefect, later achieved national fame in the 1980s by growing the world's largest leek. The claim was refuted by some who used a different standard of measurement.

Five

Events and Occasions

A WI pageant in the mid 1930s. The Women's Institute was strongly supported in both villages and went to considerable trouble to put on entertainment, both educational and humorous, for members. Through pageantry, they hoped to educate people about our history.

The old age pensioners wait in their charabanc outside the Hippodrome, Silksworth to go on their annual outing by courtesy of the management, around 1920. Mr Roland Monkhouse, of the Sunderland car firm, stands at the door.

A Daimler 'charabanc' (literally 'four on a bench'), the forerunner of today's tour coach, at another such event around 1927. Notice the bus tyres are pneumatic at the front to reduce shock on the steering wheel, but solid at the rear which only affected the passengers! The box on the step by the driver's door held the battery. A canvas hood was pulled over the passengers from the rear in wet weather, and, in the absence of a windscreen wiper, the front windscreen tilted open in the middle.

This is believed to be the Ryhope Methodist Sunday School treat which took place in Seaham Bungalow Field in 1932. Clearly, it was a happy family occasion for all, from infants to pensioners.

Ryhope children at a Methodist Sunday School treat at Seaham Hall in 1932. In those days, it was a great adventure to travel so far!

School trips were not held in wartime, and only restarted in the late 1940s. Here is a third year class from Silksworth Modern School on the sand dunes at Bamburgh. Included are, Ken Goodfellow, Arthur Rumley, Ann Bainbridge, Elsie Turnbull and Jimmy Lynn.

Silksworth Modern School trip to the Lake District, 1951. This was the annual trip when ten busloads went to the Lakes to visit Windermere and Ambleside. This group was 3A of that year and includes among others, Edward and Ronald Clark, Aaron Elves, Margaret Curry, Ann Ewington, Mary McSween, June Tinmouth, Marie Wolfendale, Eileen Johnson and Bobby Carter.

At Christmas the fourth year girls of Silksworth Modern put on entertainment for the school. This was the 'Belles of St Trinians' and includes, Sandra Nelson, Pauline Hunter, Irene Farley and Valerie Willcock (under their make-up)!

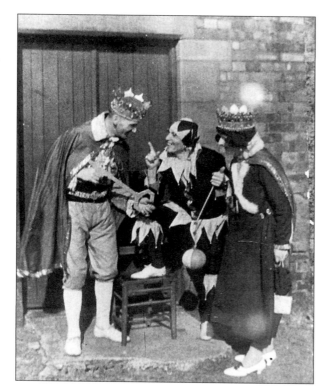

The Carnival King and Queen, 1948. The King and 'Queen' (both are male) plus the court jester were a regular feature of the fun of the village carnival. This is said to be of the personalities of Silksworth at the 1948 carnival. The 'crowning' was a much sought after distinction.

These could be the same King and Queen as in the previous photograph. They are surrounded by young 'attendants', the carnival committee, and helpers. During the hard times of the late 1920s and early '30s carnivals brought happiness, colour and fun into a depressed world in mining areas. Music was provided by gaily-dressed bands of both adults and children marching to tunes played on kazoos, a simple form of trumpet. The marching was usually of a very high standard. The Silksworth Skyliners band continued into the 1960s.

The Ryhope Carnival in 1929. Local tradesmen, colliery workers and others gave up hours of time to polish harnesses and brasses till they gleamed. Then the decorating of the carts would be a group effort, to vie for the award of 'Best decorated cart' or 'Best turn-out of the day.'

The British Legion Rag Time Band raising money for the Miners' Children's Fund in 1926. This was a common event in 1926, the year of the great Miners' Strike. The emphasis was on raising funds to support the children of the striking workers. The banner reminds villagers that the British Legion, made up of First World War ex-servicemen, was fighting for support for the cause of the miners. It used entertainment and charitable appeal in pursuit of this.

Ryhope Peace celebration, Children's Day, 6 August 1919. The celebration of the end of the First World War was all the more welcome because by then most of the servicemen had returned home, unlike the Second World War when demobilisation was spread over some three years. Local carts were pressed into service and decorated with patriotic tableaux. Everyone dressed in their best clothes, and school children played a very special part. Twenty years later many of these children were themselves in the armed forces.

VE Day celebrations, York Street, Silksworth. Street parties by the thousand were held in May 1945 to celebrate the end of the war in Europe. Everyone helped out with what they could spare, even though food was rationed and continued to be so after the victory when we helped to feed the devastated countries of Europe. The girl holding the shield is believed to be Sheila Kirtley.

The Second World War finally ended on VJ Day, 15 August 1945. The great relief of the day was celebrated with services, parades and parties. Here on the Village Green at Ryhope, a group of local youngsters laugh in the hard-won freedom of victory. Notice the old stone houses in the background between the Albion and the Forge Garage.

The unveiling of the War Memorial on Tunstall Village Green on 25 November 1922. The Green remained the site of this tribute to Silksworth war dead until around 1950, when vandals struck and broke off the soldier's bayonet. It was shortly afterwards resited in Silksworth Park for greater security and remains there to this day. The photographs are taken from a privately made home movie.

THE UNVEILING OF
THE WAR MEMORIAL
on
Tunstall Village Green
on
Saturday Nov. 25th 1922.

The War Memorial on Tunstall Green. Here it stood, in its original state, protected by spiked railings, and respected by all for some thirty years. Many of the names on the Memorial can still be found in the village today, some seventy years on from its creation. It now also carries the names of servicemen and civilians who died in the Second World War. All are honoured at the annual service of Remembrance.

The headmaster of the Ryhope Grammar School, Councillor R.P. Williams, BSc, JP, lays the foundation stone of Williams Terrace. Ryhope was originally made up of colliery houses plus a number of privately built streets such as Gray and Gordon Terrace. In the post First World War period 'council' housing had begun to provide reasonably priced accommodation for the workers who were not necessarily employed at the colliery. These streets were mostly named after councillors of the time.

The opening of Aged Miners' Homes in 1924. Homes for aged miners were needed as their right to a colliery house ended when they ceased work. The Durham Miners' Association, by a levy on its members, provided well-built and, for the time, well equipped houses, where the miner and his wife could live in comparative comfort and dignity. This group, at the opening of the Ryhope Homes, includes members of the NUM, and Durham County Miners' Association, who administered and financed the homes.

Ryhope miners had long been an organised social, as well as political, force. In 1926, on the site of the former YMCA Reading Rooms, they built the Welfare Hall, presently the Community Centre. This group, at the opening ceremony, includes Major Streatfeild, the colliery owner, in the centre wearing 'spats', and Canon P.Y. Knight, the vicar, far right wearing the mortar board.

The presentation of an ambulance trophy. The ambulance team was vital to a large colliery. Manned by highly trained volunteers, such teams competed annually for impressive trophies, cups and medals. Presentations like this one at Ryhope in the 1950s were important events. These men combined considerable skill with self-sacrificing courage when there was danger underground.

The choir leads the procession for consecration of Ryhope Cemetery extension, *c.* 1910. This shows the area very little different from today. Notice the tram inspector standing by the tram stop outside the police station, now a recently built bungalow. The extension of the cemetery marked a significant stage in the expansion of the village.

Following the choir are the church dignitaries. Canon Knight is in the centre. The top-hatted figure is Mr Tweddle, land steward for the Ryhope & Haswell Coal Company. In front of him is Harry Bell, a local builder, who converted Brick Row to two storey housing and put bedroom windows in place of skylights in the rest of the colliery houses. His son, Capt. Gordon Bell MC, is remembered by a window in St Paul's church.

The dedication of the extension to St Paul's church in 1926. As Ryhope expanded a new aisle was needed to accommodate the increase in membership of the church. This was opened and dedicated in 1926 and Canon P.Y. Knight officiated.

The Bishop of Durham, Rt Revd David Jenkins blessing the Ryhope Colliery memorial. After the closure of the colliery and the landscaping of the site as sports fields, the sacrifice of those men who died in its century or so of active life was recorded on this memorial. A miner's lamp of nineteenth century pattern hangs beside the plaque on the east wall of St Paul's church.

The dedication of a new banner for the church-run Ryhope Girls' Friendly Society in 1923.

A fund raising committee for the 1926 strike outside the Grand at Ryhope. This committee was not raising funds for the strikers but to feed the children who would otherwise suffer. This group included volunteers representing many village organisations and the local constable is prominent among them. On the notice is the headline, 'Coal v Oil'. So it was an issue even seventy years ago.

The IOGT choir, 1936. By 1936 the Independent Order of Good Templars had a very strong influence in the villages and, along with its aim to support tee-totalism, it had great influence socially. It gave young and old, a happy alternative to drink, and the unhappiness it could cause in a family. In Silksworth, in particular, it served the needs of all branches of the community for many years.

The temperance pledge of William Barnes, 10 September 1887. Drunkenness was a curse of working men in the nineteenth century. To many, the only effective alternative to harsh, underpaid working conditions was drink, so numerous temperance organisations sprang up, such as the Band of Hope and the Good Templars. They tried to attract youngsters, and adults, by asking them to 'sign the pledge' to refrain from all alcohol. They had considerable success. This is a typical certificate.

In the late 1970s a fire broke out in the yard at High Farm, Ryhope. It was effectively dealt with by Sunderland fire brigade.

Sunderland fire fighters damp down the smouldering remains of the former premises of Ryhope Co-operative Society. Having stood empty for some time, they had become a target for vandalism, and, after the fire, were completely demolished for reasons of safety. They had served generations of Ryhope families for over a century.

Six
Schooldays

Ryhope Infants group, c. 1915. The school stood opposite the old Co-op. It later become a council depot and was finally demolished to make way for the council-built houses of Western Hill. The serious expressions are possibly partly due to the need to 'keep still for the photograph' in those days.

Ryhope Infants School and attendance officer, c. 1900. With thirty-three children in the class numbers compare reasonably well with today. On the left is Alec Morris, the attendance officer, an important function when attendance determined the school allowance and the head teacher's pay. Despite his appearance he is said to have been a kindly man who did many good turns for the children in his charge.

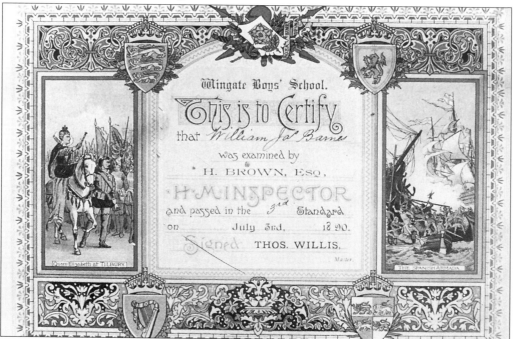

The report certificate of William Barnes, 3 July 1890. It was presented to William at Wingate School, and meant he could leave school at thirteen and take up a paid job. His parents later moved to Ryhope and provided this unique certificate.

Ryhope Infants Class *c.* 1906. Education in those days was largely a matter of desks, blackboard, chalk and talk.

Ryhope Infants, Class 1, 1910. It is interesting to notice the dress of these five-year-olds. Two boys wear collars that appear to be more suited to girls. The footwear is of poor standard, and the hair cuts look all home-done. But such was life for the families of miners almost ninety years ago. With large families most clothes were handed down from older members, and there was no point in keeping up with the neighbours, for they were in the same position.

Ryhope Infants, Class 6, 1919. The children are almost in uniform. The boys wear washable collars and the girls wear white pinafores ('pinned afore' the dresses to keep them clean). The teacher on the left wears traditional dark clothing, and the children on average seem reasonably clad.

Ryhope Infants, Class 3, 1919. Here the class size is getting bigger and the school building is becoming shabbier. Perhaps there was little or no maintenance during the First World War.

A Ryhope Boys School class of 1910. The schoolmaster is Mr Noble and this is probably the top class. In those days pupils could leave at thirteen if they achieved a satisfactory standard in the Labour Exam and go out to work. They could earn a few much needed shillings perhaps on the screens where coal and stone were sorted.

Ryhope Boys School, c. 1912. The teacher is Jack Hudson, very keen on football, and a strong disciplinarian, but nevertheless much respected over many years.

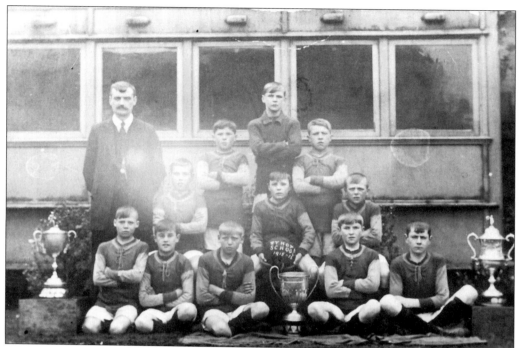

Ryhope School football team, 1915-16. Where do old trams go? Well, this one became a changing room for Ryhope School football team. The teacher is Mr J. Hudson.

A class at Ryhope Village School, c. 1900. This is probably the whole of the school with their two teachers. Many such teachers were unqualified in those days and rated as student-teachers or unqualified assistants.

Children's pageant, *c.* 1914. This is thought to be at the Ryhope Church of England School. The boy is believed to be Fred Davidson who later became a colliery manager.

Ryhope Church of England School, *c.* 1942. Three years into the Second World War this group at the Church of England School are all well turned out considering clothing was rationed. Behind them is the Parish Parlour and the Grand cinema.

A May Queen and her attendants, *c.* 1911. A rare scene inside the Church of England School, not long after its opening, probably around the time of George V's coronation. The piano was a recent acquisition. Previously, singing was done with a tuning fork which gave the starting note.

The May Queen at the Church of England School in 1929. Every year a May Queen was chosen from the older pupils and duly garlanded for the coronation with her attendants. Such events brightened the otherwise uneventful routine of daily life, and became incidents to remember in one's life.

A May Queen and her attendants in 1937. Another coronation year, that of George VI and Queen Elizabeth. The Queen is Freda Thompson.

H. Hepburn of Ryhope Senior (later Modern) School in 1937. He is with his silver cup as 'Victor Ludorum', a Latin title borrowed from public schools meaning 'school champion'. Excellence in sport was recognised by almost every school by the 1930s.

Cauld Knuckles School in the mid 1930s. The quaintly named 'Cauld Knuckles' School was built by the Coal Company to serve families on 'The Hill' at Ryhope. The area was also called Vinegar Hill, after an acrimonious battle in Ireland in the late eighteenth century and was named because of the many Irish immigrants who settled there.

The old Village School, Silksworth. The village was originally a small farming community at the bottom of Botcherby's Bank and had a school as far back as the 1850s in Church of England premises. New Silksworth, i.e. the present village, sprang up with the development and expansion of the colliery of Lord Londonderry. The Village School initially served mainly children of farm workers. It remained open until the late 1950s, then was converted into a private dwelling by a local farmer. An inspector's report of over a century ago commented: 'The girls' out-offices were scribbled on in an offensive manner, and there was an inadequate supply of ashes for the boys.' Ashes were a convenient way of covering the unpleasant contents of the earth-closest.

A class of five-year-olds at Silksworth Infants School with their teacher, c. 1950.

Silksworth Juniors, c. 1911. Silksworth Junior School was built in the 1870s to serve the older children of the village. Note the popularity of white rubber collars.

New Silksworth Juniors, Class 1, 1951.

Silksworth Juniors football team, 1953-54. Back row: Mr Gormley, Mr Kirk, Mr Woolcock. Middle row: Carr, Appleby, Clark, Maynard, Carlin, Laverick. Front row: Surtees, Jackson, Winlow, Nicholson, Raeper. The boys were League champions and winners of the Hedworth and RAOB cups.

Silksworth Juniors, 1964-65, winners of the RAOB cup. Back row: Mr Gormley, Rumford, Robinson, Reay. Middle row: Swindle, Widdrington, Bunker, Gray, Jones, Blyth. Front row: Clennell, Sproates, Robinson, Harrison, Longstaff.

Silksworth Modern School, second years, c. 1950. They include, Margaret Curry, Sylvia Swinburne, Jimmy Pearson and Lawrence Carr. The teacher is Mr Groves.

Silksworth pupils from the 1960s. Around 1960 'winkle-picker shoes' were the fashion, as can be seen in the front row. The group includes, Leslie Dunn, Keith Grose, Janice Mould (later school secretary), Marjorie France, Robert Joyce, Alan Teare and Brian Lamb.

Silksworth Modern School Christmas party, 1949. This photograph was taken by flash 'powder' by the author. Flashbulbs were rare for the amateur photographer. The room was darkened, camera shutter opened, flash powder ignited and camera shutter closed. Hence the variety of surprised and terrified expressions. After 1947, parties were held in the school hall four nights of the week at Christmas. Entertainment was a mixture of games and dances including, the 'Bradford Barn', 'Military 2-step', and 'Dashing White Sergeant', all learned in school time. A group of senior pupils helped Miss Lowe, the cookery teacher, to lay the tables and clear away and wash up each night. This group includes John Brown, Dempster Johnson, Audrey Stelling and Sally Donnelly.

A group of 3A pupils pose in their home-made party hats, specially designed for the occasion. The group includes, Norman Richardson, Gloria Ruddick and Sonia Marshall.

There was no disco dancing in the mid 1950s. The dances learned in country dancing lessons were very lively, and all joined in with great gusto. This was the 'Dashing White Sergeant'. The teacher on the right in the black suit was Mr Poulter, who later became a vicar in Sunderland.

Billy Dunn and Susan Mycock among others, in the ever popular 'Bradford Barn Dance'. One changed partners every few bars, which was useful, if you got a partner with two left feet.

Two fourth year girls demonstrate the beginnings of the 'Rock and Roll' era, quite a revolution for those days.

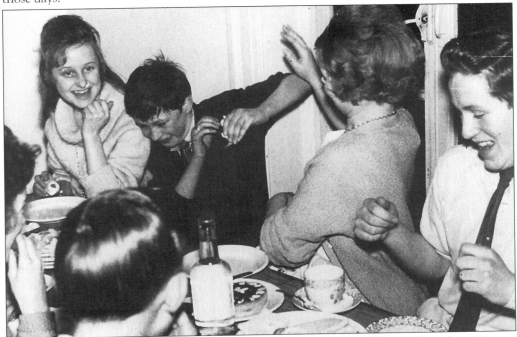

Good behaviour at the table for the Christmas party was enforced by the 'gentle sex' in no uncertain manner. Sandra is here striking a blow for women's lib.

A Silksworth class enjoy their school milk in the 1950s. Morning break was the time for a one third pint bottle of milk and a straw. Served in the classroom, it was generally hastily consumed before dashing into the playground for a brief game of football. Ron Clark, John Cowie and Ivan Gunn appear in this group.

A cookery class from Silksworth, in the obligatory hats and aprons, around 1948. The group includes, Alice Robinson, Norma Laverick, Frances Fairley, Doris Milner, Irene Scott, Gloria Allen, Doris Young and Janet Walton.

A group of Silksworth girls producing craft work in plastic in the 1950s. At the time, Silksworth was the only school in the county doing such work. The group includes, Betsy Mycock and Elizabeth Ayre.

Specimens of 'thrown' pots (i.e. produced by throwing clay on a potter's wheel) made under the tuition of Mr Mason at Silksworth Modern School. The school had a county-wide reputation for this craft in the 1950s.

In 1956 Silksworth Modern School was chosen to enter a display on British Friesian Cattle for the National Show of the Royal Agricultural Society, held that year on the Town Moor at Newcastle and again in a subsequent year. A party from the top year went for the day. The group on the tractor includes, Beryl McArthur, Colin Harvey, Sandra Bainbridge, Evelyn Bowdon and Peter Mycock.

Young gardeners from Silksworth in 1949. Left to right: Brown, Boal, Surtees, Collins and Cutting. After the 'Dig for Victory' slogan of wartime, school gardening was on the timetable. The Silksworth Modern School garden was on the site of the present Health Centre. Here, in 1949, third year boys go to work. They were often supervised by passing pensioners from over the fence, who freely supplied advice, criticism and occasionally rather choice language.

Silksworth boys Brian Simpson and Peter France are in this choir practice group from the 1950s. The music teacher, Mr Fox, was also a church organist and choir master, and these boys benefited from his training in the early 1960s.

The girls from Mr Fox's choir group practising, we believe, in St Matthew's church.

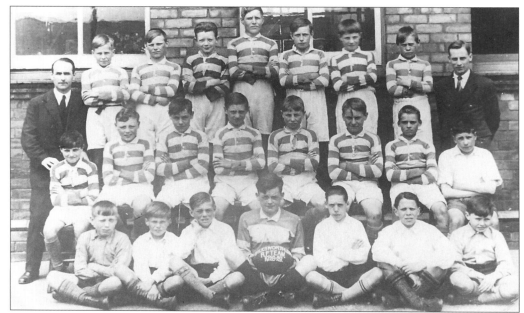

Silksworth Secondary rugby team, 1928-29. At this time rugby was enjoying a spell of popularity under Mr Leith, on the left. He served at the school from 1908-47, apart from his time in the army during the First World War. For the time these boys are very well dressed in proper strips but none are wearing football boots.

Silksworth School football team, 1948-49. The team includes, W. Bainbridge (captain), G. Stones, F. Swinburne, F. Pace and G. Lax.

Silksworth School football team, September 1949. After the war the school expanded with the raising of the leaving age to fifteen. Junior and senior football teams were run by Mr Flaxen and Mr Mason respectively. Both teachers gave many years of loyal service and encouragement to young footballers, achieving great success. The team includes, Dobbinson, Lumley, Bond and Crooks.

Silksworth senior boys football team, 1951. The teacher is Mr Mason and the captain David Dimond. Included, among others, are Ronnie Clark, Raymond Pace, George Harwood and David Mycock.

The successful Silksworth side of 1956.
Peter Simpson was captain while the
others include, Alan Whitwham
(goalkeeper), David Lemon, Norman
Barron and Robert Davidson.

Silksworth Junior (or 'A') team run by Mr Flaxen, 1961-62. Among others are, Harry Crabtree
(captain), Tony Wales and Alan Teare.

110

Silksworth Secondary Modern cricket team, 1950. The captain was E. Clark and the vice-captain was F. Gannon. G. Bedell, holding the board, was the wicket keeper. The opening batsmen were F. Pace and A. Rumney.

Silksworth Modern cricket team, 1956. Included are, Alan Donaldson, Norman Barron, George Laverick and Stanley Mould.

Silksworth School netball team, September 1949. Netball was encouraged in post-war years under Miss Balderstone. While the girls played for a successful result, good sportsmanship was always looked on as the first requirement. The team of 1949 was captained by Iris Forth and included Moira Donnelly and Sheila Chapman.

Silksworth School netball team, 1951-52. The young ladies include, Maureen Patton, Shirley Logan, Jean Guy and Margaret Curry. Their teacher is, as ever, Miss Balderstone.

Silksworth netball team, 1957-58, captained by Norma Anderson. Other members include, Ann Collins, Esther Turbin, Sandra Hammond and Marjorie Tait.

Silksworth netball team, November 1963. They were trained by Miss Baird, at the rear. The team includes, Sheila Davidson and Ann Newton.

A Silksworth School trip in the 1950s. The group includes, Shirley Gillespie, Elsie Turnbull, Pat Mycock, Arthur Rumley, Fred Pace, Ken Goodfellow and Hazel Palmer.

Class 3A at their Christmas party in 1955. This Silksworth group includes, Alan Bell, George Smillie, Alan Douglas, Sheila Appleby, Vera Green, Nancy Harris and Olive Glass.

Seven
People

County Councillor Wilkie Lumley of Ryhope (standing left), at an old age pensioners' Christmas dinner in the 1940s. His son Arthur also became a Councillor, and, ultimately, Mayor of Sunderland.

Around 1949 Ryhope Co-op began replacing butcher's carts with Ford vans. Sid Lorraine was one of the first drivers, seen here with his van.

The Oriental Bar, c. 1912. The name of Maggiore was well known in Ryhope until quite recently. The shop was often also known as 'Jocks' or 'Louis'. It ceased to be an ice-cream shop with the death of the last member of the family, Evo Maggiore, in the 1980s.

In the closing years of the nineteenth century a fire devastated the houses in Cory Street, Ryhope, with the blaze travelling along the roof space.

During the fire a baby was rescued and, wrapped in blankets, laid at the bottom of the long garden. The infant was Edward Summers. As an adult, he emigrated to South Africa and became mayor of the town of Brakpan. During the Second World War he sent food parcels to the old folk of Ryhope in gratitude for his deliverance some forty years earlier. Here he wears his chain of office.

Deaconess Cowens served St Paul's church members for many years. This photograph would seem to be from around 1920 and was perhaps taken in the vicarage garden.

A vicarage group in Edwardian Times. The photograph was taken at a St Paul's church garden party. Canon P.Y. Knight is fifth from the right at the rear.

A Ryhope wedding group of the early 1920s. For its day this was a very formal and elaborate group. Notice the 'Happy Couple'. The strain of waiting for the camera to click was probably too much.

Members of Taylor Street chapel, c. 1934. Taylor Street chapel served people living on 'The Hill', an area now covered by local authority housing.

A group of the Ryhope Lodge of Oddfellows. Temperance organisations were a direct result of over-indulgence in alcohol in Victorian times. The regalia did much to attract members.

J. Frecker's fruit cart, 1914. 'Flat' carts were light in weight, easy to turn in a street, and had a 'platform' at a convenient height for handling produce. Notice the polished shine on the driver's boots and the harness and hooves of the horse. Pride of turnout was looked on as important in those days too.

A Binns van driven by Mr Wrigglesworth, c. 1920. Mr Wrigglesworth lived in Ryhope and was a driver and chauffeur for Binns for many years. Notice the spare tyre (but not wheel) and the long bull horn. In those days Binns were just 'drapers' and not the huge department store they later became.

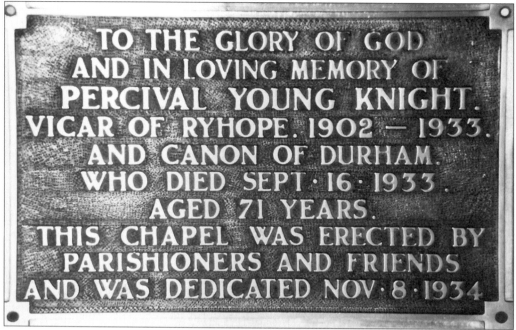

TO THE GLORY OF GOD
AND IN LOVING MEMORY OF
PERCIVAL YOUNG KNIGHT.
VICAR OF RYHOPE. 1902 — 1933.
AND CANON OF DURHAM.
WHO DIED SEPT · 16 · 1933.
AGED 71 YEARS.
THIS CHAPEL WAS ERECTED BY
PARISHIONERS AND FRIENDS
AND WAS DEDICATED NOV · 8 · 1934

The memorial to Canon Percival Young Knight who was a faithful vicar for thirty-one years. A man of strong character and fearlessly frank, he was respected by the majority of the population.

A reunion dinner of Ryhope old comrades in the 1930s.

Councillor W. Lumley (centre) and representatives of the Durham Branch of the NUM at Leechmere Hall in the 1940s. The Hall later became a centre for aged miners, before being demolished to make room for Council housing.

Ryhope Labour party, Women's Section, c. 1936. The Labour Party was always a strong force in a mining village. Among these supporters of the Women's Section is Mrs Dot Ridley, third from the left, who gave a lifetime of service to local politics and the people as a councillor.

To the memory of Pilot Officer Cyril Joe Barton V.C. (168669) R.A.F.V. No.578 Squadron who died on the 31st March 1944, after crash-landing hi crippled Halifax bomber south west of Hollycarrside, thus avoiding Ryhop

He displayed unsurpassed courage and devotion to duty, then sacrifice his life to save others and was posthumously awarded the Victoria Cros

Pilot Officer C.J. Barton VC is remembered on the Ryhope War Memorial. His Halifax bomber crashed at Hollycarrside in 1944, and by remaining at the controls to the last, he avoided causing many deaths. For this he became Ryhope's hero and was awarded a posthumous Victoria Cross.

A group of Silksworth men, due to the fortunes of war, found themselves in a company of the 7th Battalion Somerset Light Infantry. The seated soldier, on the right with the crossed flags, was probably a semaphore signaller.

'Just like Dad', 1917. In those days he wouldn't know if Dad would ever return home from that horrific conflict.

Knitting comforts for the troops in 1940. The women are outside Cauld Knuckles School, which was by then vacated, and used as a wartime centre. The ladies of Ryhope, like those in every town and village, knitted socks, gloves, scarves and balaclava helmets for the forces. Such gifts were sent to every theatre of Operations. Even the African desert could be very cold at night.

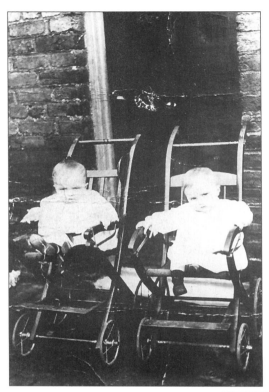

Two babies in pushchairs in 1921. These were the latest in folding pushchairs, heavy and solidly made to outlast several generations.

Two young girls in Stewart Street in 1930. The push chair is obviously home-made, using a pair of wheels from an old pram, but it served its purpose. One of these children, we understand, became a teacher at Silksworth Modern School, the late Mrs Keirl.

These children from 1914 are dressed in strong boots, strong coats and headgear, influenced by the First World War. This, and other similar photographs, were probably taken by Mr Bradwell, who had his studio at the bottom of Cliff Road, Ryhope at the time of the war, when few working folk had cameras.

Jim Pace with his class 3A, Silksworth Modern School, 1952-3.

Jim Pace at the permanent exhibition of his photographs at Ryhope Health Centre. This unique 'wall of history' was put in the entrance of the Health Centre in February 1987 as a public memorial to Dr Ronald Henderson, for many years a respected GP in the village.